WHAT IS THE JUDICIAL BRANCH?

LAURA LORIA

Britannica®
Educational Publishing

IN ASSOCIATION WITH

ROSEN
EDUCATIONAL SERVICES

Published in 2016 by Britannica Educational Publishing (a trademark of Encyclopædia Britannica, Inc.) in association with The Rosen Publishing Group, Inc.
29 East 21st Street, New York, NY 10010

Distributed exclusively by Rosen Publishing.
To see additional Britannica Educational Publishing titles, go to rosenpublishing.com.

First Edition

Britannica Educational Publishing
J.E. Luebering: Director, Core Reference Group
Mary Rose McCudden: Editor, Britannica Student Encyclopedia

Rosen Publishing
Hope Lourie Killcoyne: Executive Editor
Amelie von Zumbusch: Editor
Nelson Sá: Art Director
Danijah Brevard: Designer
Cindy Reiman: Photography Manager

Library of Congress Cataloging-in-Publication Data

Loria, Laura, author.
What is the judicial branch?/Laura Loria. — First edition.
    pages cm. — (Let's find out! Government)
Includes bibliographical references and index.
ISBN 978-1-62275-961-3 (library bound) — ISBN 978-1-62275-962-0 (pbk.) —
ISBN 978-1-62275-964-4 (6-pack)
1. Courts — United States — Juvenile literature. I. Title.
KF8720.L67 2016
347.73'2 — dc23

2014037709

Manufactured in the United States of America

Photo credits: Cover, p. 1 © iStockphoto.com/trekandshoot; p. 4 © iStockphoto.com/IS_ImageSource; p. 5 Orhan Cam/Shutterstock.com; p. 6 Kids.gov; pp. 7, 9, 19, 20 © AP Images; p. 8 Clarence Holmes/age fotostock/SuperStock; pp. 10, 14 The Washington Post/Getty Images; pp. 11, 18, 21, 22 Library of Congress Prints and Photographs Division Washington, D.C.; p. 12 Bloomberg/Getty Images; p. 13 Stephen Jaffe/AFP/Getty Images; p. 15 Bruce Gifford/Moment Mobile/Getty Images; p. 16 Deborah Coleman/Getty Images; p. 17 © Richard Hutchings/PhotoEdit; p. 23 Carl Iwasaki/The Life Images Collection/Getty Images; p. 24 Hulton Archive/Getty Images; p. 25 Hank Walker/The Life Picture Collection/Getty Images; p. 26 David Hume Kennerly/Getty Images; p. 27 Mark Wilson/Getty Images; p. 28 Jose Luis Magana/Reuters/Landov; p. 29 Martin Dallaire/Shutterstock.com; interior pages background image Uyen Le/Photodisc/Getty Images

CONTENTS

Justice for All

Many children say the Pledge of Allegiance every morning at school. The last line is "with liberty and justice for all." Liberty means freedom, but what does justice mean? Justice means making sure that laws are interpreted correctly and that people are treated fairly.

The judicial branch of the United States government is a system of courts. The courts decide if laws are just and if people have broken the law. Sometimes people go to court when laws are broken. In the

Lawyers call witnesses to help prove their side of a case in court.

court, lawyers argue two sides of a story. A judge watches over everything. In some cases, a jury decides if a person is guilty or innocent. In other cases, courts make decisions about the laws themselves.

Each state has its own judicial system. Above that is the federal court system. The federal courts handle legal cases that affect the national government. The most powerful court in the country is the Supreme Court.

The Supreme Court meets in this building in Washington, D.C.

5

THE CONSTITUTION

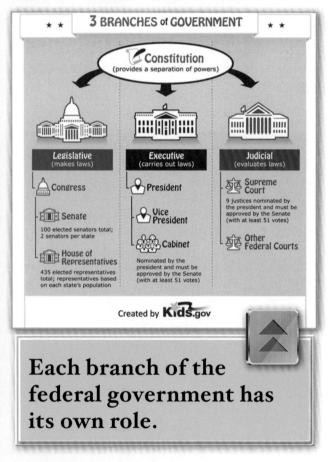

3 BRANCHES of GOVERNMENT ★ ★

Constitution
(provides a separation of powers)

Legislative
(makes laws)

Congress

Senate
100 elected senators total;
2 senators per state

House of
Representatives
435 elected representatives
total; representatives based
on each state's population

Executive
(carries out laws)

President

Vice
President

Cabinet
Nominated by the
president and must be
approved by the Senate
(with at least 51 votes)

Judicial
(evaluates laws)

Supreme
Court
9 justices nominated by
the president and must be
approved by the Senate
(with at least 51 votes)

Other
Federal Courts

Created by **Kids**.gov

Each branch of the federal government has its own role.

When the United States was being formed, its leaders wrote a document to spell out how its government would work. This document is called the Constitution. The Constitution calls for three equal branches of federal government: executive, legislative, and judicial. The leader of the executive branch is the president. The House of Representatives and the Senate make up the legislative branch.

President Barack Obama nominated Patricia Ann Millett to be a federal judge in 2013.

The judicial branch uses the U.S. Constitution and other laws of the U.S. government to settle cases. It can also strike down a law passed by Congress if the Supreme Court declares that it goes against the Constitution. If the president makes an order that is unconstitutional, the Supreme Court can stop that, too.

The other branches have some power over the judicial branch. The president nominates, or proposes, all federal judges. The nominees then have to be approved by the Senate.

LOWER COURTS

More than 300 million people live in the United States. The Supreme Court cannot possibly decide all of the cases that need to be heard. The lower courts do much of the work of the judicial branch.

District courts are the lowest level of federal courts. There are 94 of these courts in the United States. These are separated into 12 groups, called circuits.

A person who loses a case in a district court can appeal the decision in a court of appeals. There are

This district court in White Plains, New York, is part of the Second Circuit.

The judges on a panel work together to make decisions, using their combined knowledge and experience.

12 of these courts, one for each circuit. Panels, or groups, of judges usually hear cases in courts of appeals. They have the power to overturn, or undo, the judgments of the lower courts.

VOCABULARY

To **appeal** a case is to ask for a higher court to think about the case and make a new decision.

THE SUPREME COURT

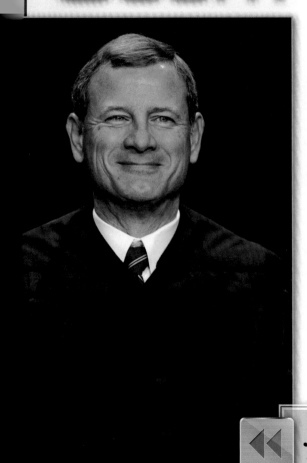

The Supreme Court is the highest court in the United States. The nine judges on the Supreme Court are called justices. The leader is called the chief justice. The others are associate justices. When the justices decide a case, each person has an equal say. Some of their decisions are very close, with five members voting one way and four voting the other way.

John Roberts was appointed the Supreme Court's chief justice in 2005.

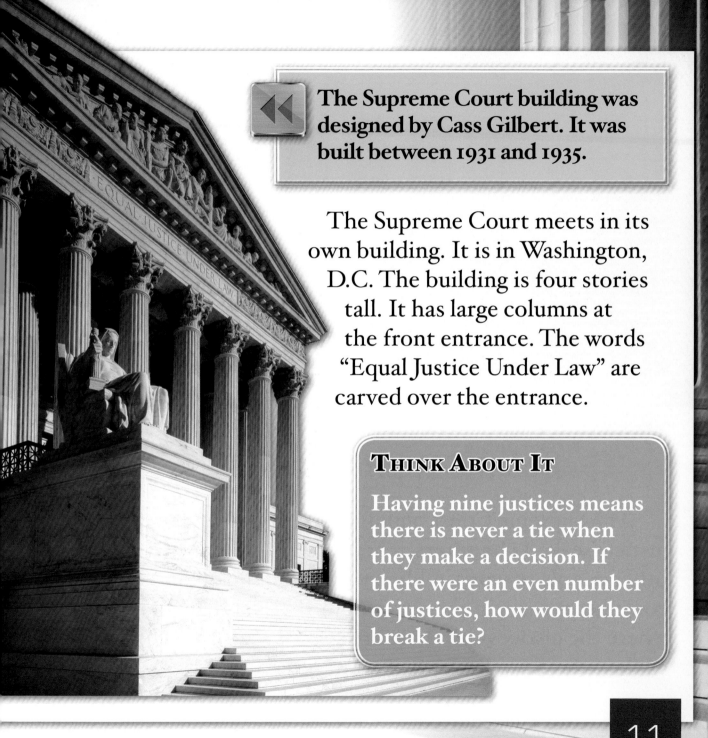

The Supreme Court building was designed by Cass Gilbert. It was built between 1931 and 1935.

The Supreme Court meets in its own building. It is in Washington, D.C. The building is four stories tall. It has large columns at the front entrance. The words "Equal Justice Under Law" are carved over the entrance.

THINK ABOUT IT

Having nine justices means there is never a tie when they make a decision. If there were an even number of justices, how would they break a tie?

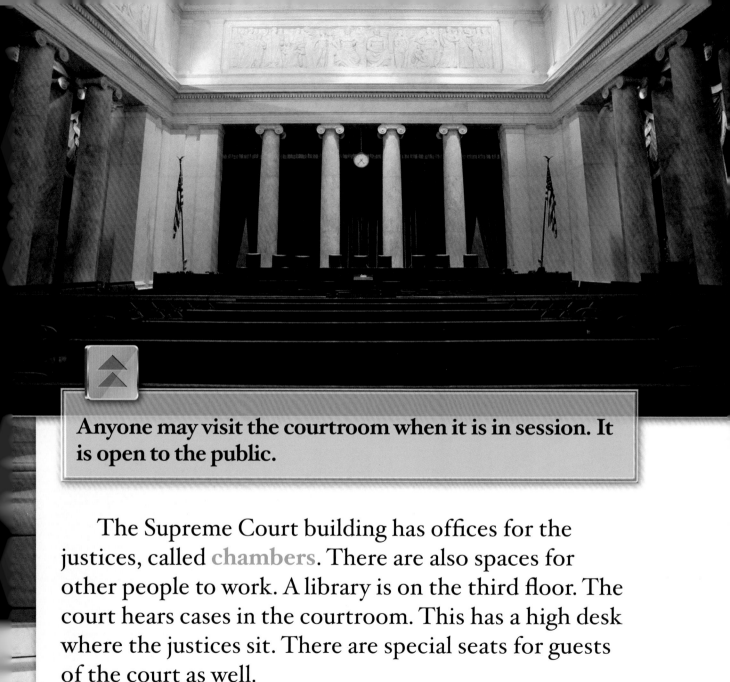

Anyone may visit the courtroom when it is in session. It is open to the public.

The Supreme Court building has offices for the justices, called chambers. There are also spaces for other people to work. A library is on the third floor. The court hears cases in the courtroom. This has a high desk where the justices sit. There are special seats for guests of the court as well.

The justices need many people to help them run the court. They are called court officers. The court clerk keeps track of the calendars and schedules. The court marshal is responsible for security, as well as keeping the court on time. The marshal uses colored signals to tell lawyers when their time is up. Librarians, lawyers, and computer officers also help the Supreme Court. The justices choose the court officers.

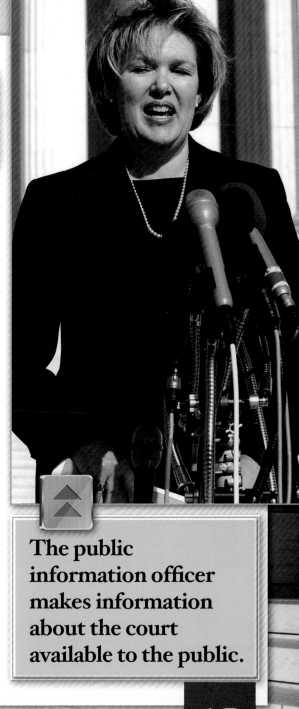

The public information officer makes information about the court available to the public.

Choosing Judges

The president of the United States nominates all federal judges. The president picks a person who has excellent knowledge of the law. Most presidents choose nominees who think like they do or whom they have worked with before.

Senators asked Elena Kagan questions from June 28 to 30, 2010. On August 5, she was confirmed as a Supreme Court justice.

After the president nominates a person, the Senate must approve that choice. First, a small group, called a committee, has a hearing. Committee members ask nominees about their thoughts on the law. After the committee votes on the nominee, the whole Senate votes. A nominee must gain at least 51 votes from the 100 senators in order to become a judge.

Two days after her confirmation, Elena Kagan was sworn in as a Supreme Court justice.

How state court judges are selected varies from state to state. In some states, judges are elected. In others, the governor or a legislative committee appoints judges. Appointed judges generally need voter approval to keep their jobs.

COMPARE AND CONTRAST
In Maine, the governor appoints state court judges. In Ohio, they are elected. What are the advantages of each system?

FEDERAL COURTS AND STATE COURTS

Different kinds of cases are tried in federal courts than in state courts. Cases that deal with whether a law is permitted by the Constitution are tried in federal court. So are disputes between states. Federal courts hear all bankruptcy cases.

Most criminal cases, such as robbery cases, are tried in state courts. Family law cases, such as those about divorces and adoptions, also take place in state courts. State courts deal

Federal and state courts follow many of the same rules and procedures.

Family court judges also rule on how children will divide their time between divorced parents.

with personal injury cases, as well as with cases involving the wills of people who have died. The ruling of a state trial court can be appealed to a higher state court. A decision from the highest state court can be appealed to the U. S. Supreme Court.

VOCABULARY
People or businesses that are deep in debt can declare **bankruptcy** to get a fresh start.

DECIDING CASES

While judges decide some lower-court cases, juries decide others. During a trial, jury members listen carefully to the arguments that each side's lawyers make. Then the jury discusses the case in private until all of the members agree on a decision in the case.

In Supreme Court cases, there are no witnesses and there is no jury. After lawyers for both sides make their arguments, the justices meet in private to make a decision. A majority of the justices must agree before the court can make its decision.

John Marshall Harlan (right) was an associate justice on the Supreme Court in the late 1800s.

COMPARE AND CONTRAST

People on a jury must all agree on a decision. The Supreme Court can disagree when it makes a decision. What are the advantages of each method?

One justice writes a statement called an opinion to explain the decision. Justices who disagree with the decision can write their own opinions, which are called dissenting opinions. Judges on lower courts often use Supreme Court opinions to decide later cases.

Lawyers have an hour to present their side of a case to the Supreme Court.

Key Supreme Court Decisions

The Supreme Court hears many cases. The most important of these have become known as landmark cases. The decisions that came from these cases changed American history.

One famous example of a landmark case is *Marbury v.*

Supreme Court justices serve until they die or retire.

James Madison was part of President Thomas Jefferson's cabinet when he was named in *Marbury v. Madison.*

PORTRAITS OF THE PRESIDENTS.

JAMES MADISON,
4ᵗʰ PRESIDENT OF THE UNITED STATES.

PHILADELPHIA.

Published by C. S. WILLIAMS, N.E. corner of Market & 7ᵗʰ St.

Madison, a case from 1803. The Constitution does not explain how to determine if a law that Congress has passed goes against the Constitution. Chief Justice John Marshall's decision in *Marbury v. Madison* stated that this is the Supreme Court's job. It set a precedent that the Supreme Court would decide whether laws were constitutional or not. This power is called judicial review.

Vocabulary

A **precedent** sets an example for how things will be done in the future.

"Separate but equal" schools, restrooms, and train cars for blacks and whites were legal at one time in the United States.

Plessy v. Ferguson was another famous Supreme Court decision. It allowed for segregation, or the forced separation of blacks and whites in public places. Homer Plessy was part white and part black. Plessy was arrested when he refused to ride in a train car set aside for African Americans. He appealed his case all the way to

THINK ABOUT IT

The Supreme Court went against one of its own rulings. Is it a good idea for the government to admit when it is wrong and change its mind?

the Supreme Court. Plessy argued that separate cars for African Americans and whites were unconstitutional. The court disagreed with him.

A later court reversed that decision. It decided that segregation was wrong. In *Brown v. Board of Education of Topeka*, it ruled that having separate schools for white and African American children was unconstitutional. That led to other courts ruling against unfair laws.

When Linda Brown was not allowed to go to this school for white children, her parents took their case to the Supreme Court and won.

Famous Supreme Court Justices

All Supreme Court justices have done important things, but there are a few who stand out. One is John Marshall. Marshall was the fourth chief justice of the Supreme Court. He served for 34 years, longer than anyone else. Before joining the court, he had served in his state legislature, in Congress, and as secretary of state. His first important case was

 John Marshall heard more than 1,000 cases during his time on the Supreme Court.

Marbury v. Madison. This changed how the court works, giving it more power than it had before.

Thurgood Marshall was the first African American justice on the Supreme Court. Before he was on the court, he argued cases before the court as a lawyer. His early work included his winning argument in the case of *Brown v. Board of Education of Topeka.* He was a strong supporter of equal rights for all U.S. citizens. In 1967 he was appointed to the court. He served for 24 years before retiring.

VOCABULARY

The **secretary of state** helps the president deal with foreign countries.

After retiring, Sandra Day O'Connor wrote several books, including one about the history of the Supreme Court.

The first woman to serve as a Supreme Court justice was Sandra Day O'Connor. She joined the court in 1981. Very few women were lawyers or judges when she graduated from law school. She worked her way up in government. She served as a lawmaker and a judge in Arizona.

Sonia Sotomayor is the first Hispanic justice, as well as the third woman,

Sonia Sotomayor was President Barack Obama's first Supreme Court nominee.

to serve on the Supreme Court. She had been a district-court judge in New York. Later, she became a judge for an appeals court. She was confirmed as a justice in 2009.

Think About It

The Supreme Court has become more diverse over time. Why is that important for justice?

Guaranteeing Justice

Every year, the Supreme Court hears cases about important issues. The court's decisions can affect every American. While the decisions of lower courts may not have the same sweeping impact, they have a huge effect on the lives of the people involved in each case.

The judicial branch has an important job. Though our country has gotten better at treating its people fairly, the judicial branch must always watch out for the people. It must make sure that anybody

People protest in front of the Supreme Court. The court's decisions can cause great changes.

This statue, called *Contemplation of Justice*, sits outside of the Supreme Court building.

who is accused of a crime gets a fair trial. Settling disputes between people fairly is another part of the judicial branch's job, as is making sure that our laws are in keeping with the Constitution, which guarantees justice and freedom for all.

COMPARE AND CONTRAST

How are the roles of the Supreme Court and the lower courts different? How are they alike?

GLOSSARY

appoints Officially names.

confirmed Approved.

criminal Having to do with things that are against the law.

disputes Disagreements about matters.

diverse Made up of things or people who are different from each other.

document An official paper relied on as the basis, proof, or support of something.

elected Voted into office.

guarantees Promises to provide.

interpreted Explained the meaning of something.

jury A group of people who make a decision in a legal case.

justice Fair treatment, in particular fair treatment under the law.

landmark A development that marks a turning point.

majority A number greater than half.

nominates Chooses someone for a job, position, office, or so forth.

opinion A formal statement by a judge or court, explaining the reasons a decision was made according to the law.

rights Things that a person is or should be morally or legally allowed to have, get, or do.

ruling An official decision made by a judge or other authority.

trial The hearing of a case in court.

witnesses People who make statements in court about what they know or have seen.

For More Information

Books

Barnes, Peter W., and Cheryl S. Barnes. *Marshall, the Courthouse Mouse: A Tail of the U.S. Supreme Court*. Washington, DC: Little Patriot Press, 2012.

DiPrimio, Pete. *The Judicial Branch* (My Guide to the Constitution). Hockessin, DE: Mitchell Lane Publishers, 2011.

Rodger, Ellen. *What Is the Judicial Branch?* (Your Guide to Government). New York, NY: Crabtree Publishing, 2013.

Taylor-Butler, Christine. *The Supreme Court* (True Books: American History). Danbury, CT: Children's Press, 2008.

Winter, Jonah. *Sonia Sotomayor: A Judge Grows in the Bronx.* New York, NY: Atheneum Books for Young Readers, 2009.

Websites

Because of the changing nature of Internet links, Rosen Publishing has developed an online list of websites related to the subject of this book. This site is updated regularly. Please use this link to access the list:

http://www.rosenlinks.com/LFO/Jud

INDEX